PAINTINGS IN LIGHT

For over a thousand years, glass artists have 'painted with light', filling our cathedrals and churches with beautiful works of art.

Stained glass windows

GW00643588

closer to God.

Canterbury Cathedral has some of the oldest and finest stained glass windows in Europe. Many windows are of international historical importance and work goes on today to preserve them so that future generations can appreciate them too.

I hope you enjoy reading all about these amazing windows, and seeing them up close for yourself!

Martyn Barr

ps. £1 from every copy of this book sold goes to the cathedral's restoration appeal.
pps. You might find binoculars useful as you walk round!

Written and designed by Martyn Barr.

Published by Out of the Box Publishing Limited in association with Canterbury Cathedral.

Consultants: Léonie Seliger, Director of Stained Glass, Canterbury Cathedral, and Bob Newport, Professor of Materials Physics, University of Kent.

This book is dedicated to the thousands of artisans and craftsmen who created this amazing cathedral and those who work so hard now to keep it looking beautiful.

A BRIEF HISTORY OF GLASS

Glass is an amazing substance! It can be clear or coloured, transparent or opaque, durable or fragile... and often very beautiful. Today, it is used in so many different ways it is hard to imagine a world without glass.

Archaeologists believe that the first man-made glass was produced in the Bronze Age around 4,000 years ago in what is now Iraq and northern Syria. It was made from the simplest of ingredients – a mixture of sand, soda or potash and lime (the chemical compound calcium oxide, not the green fruit!).

Soda or potash lowers the temperature at which the sand melts, making glass easier to produce, and calcium makes the mixture more workable. Depending on when and where the glass was made, soda came in the form of the natural mineral trona – or natron – or as ash from burnt seaweed. In Europe, potash was made by burning beech leaves or ferns.

When these three ingredients are heated to 1,000–1,100 °C they become soft and syrupy and the molten glass can be easily shaped and moulded. As the glass cools, it solidifies, maintaining its shape.

◀ Glass occurs in nature too. Obsidian, for example, is produced by volcanoes.

▲ Glassmakers inflate glass like a balloon to shape and mould it.

Heating up something to such high temperatures was a challenge for Bronze Age glassmakers. Furnaces were small and so only a small amount of glass could be produced at a time. This small scale of production, and the skills and knowledge required by the glassmakers, meant that glass objects were highly valued... and expensive.

Glassmaking was transformed in the first century BC with the discovery of glass blowing by the Romans. By blowing into

▸ Glass is heated in a furnace to 1,000–1,100 °C until it becomes soft and syrupy.

◀ Fibre-optic cables are made up of strands of an amazingly pure glass as thin as a human hair. They can carry huge amounts of digital information over long distances.

a ball of molten glass through a long metal tube, glassmakers realised they could inflate it like a balloon. This could be shaped with tools or blown into a decorated mould. Metal oxide powders were added to create colours. Copper, for example, produced blue, green or opaque red glass, depending on the conditions in the furnace. Manganese produced a purple glass, chrome green and cobalt a beautiful blue.

With the invention of larger furnaces, glass could be mass produced quickly and cheaply, and demand increased substantially. The Romans made the world's first window panes and decorated the inside of their buildings with glass panels and mosaics.

The three main ingredients in glass stayed much the same for thousands of years until the discovery of lead crystal glass in the 17th century. Over time, new techniques for making and decorating glass developed. Craftsmen created ever more complex and beautiful objects and scientists found new ways of using glass to assist in their discoveries.

In the late 1950s, a new method for manufacturing large sheets of flat glass was invented in Britain. Most windows today are made using this float glass process.

Today, glass has a huge variety of uses, from cookware and computer displays to car windscreens and telescopes. It can even be spun into fibres for telephone cables or woven into a ceramic hybrid fabric to create heat shields for spacecraft.

▼ Spacecraft have heat shields to protect them from the extremely high temperatures encountered during re-entry. Glass is a key component in these.

7

HOW A STAINED GLASS WINDOW IS MADE

The way a stained glass window is made has changed little over the centuries. After the subject and location were agreed between the church leaders and the donor – the person paying for the window – the glazier would come up with a sketch design called a 'vidimus'. If everyone was happy, the design would be copied on to a whitewashed table top (today, glaziers use paper, but in medieval times it was much too expensive!).

The full size design showed the location of the lead lines that would hold the individual pieces of glass together, as well as the colours of the pieces and any additional painting that would be required. It was a bit like a giant 'painting by numbers' picture!

One advantage of this approach is that designs could be reused in other locations. Sometimes they were even used again in the same building, but turned around or with small changes in colour and detail.

Glass-making and glazing were two separate occupations. The coloured glass usually came from Europe, particularly Northern France, though clear glass was made closer to home in Sussex and Surrey.

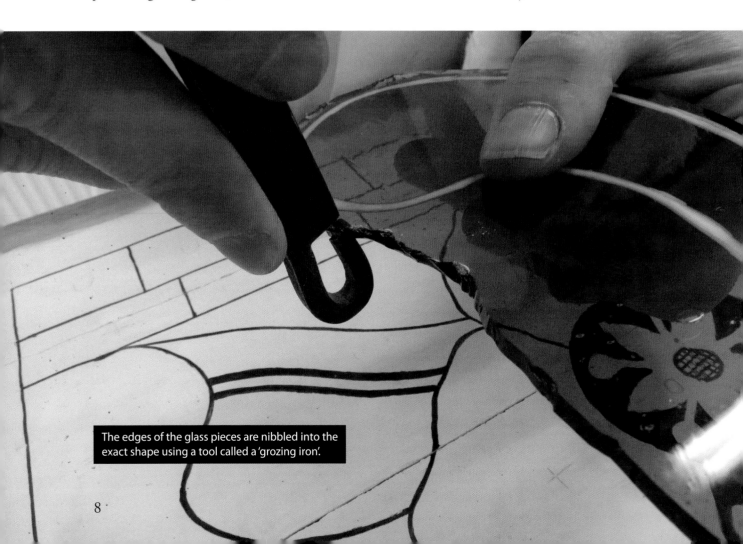

The edges of the glass pieces are nibbled into the exact shape using a tool called a 'grozing iron'.

8

The design is carefully painted on to the glass using the drawing below as a template.

The glass-maker gathered a ball of molten glass on the end of a long hollow rod, then blew it into a bottle shape. This was then cut off at each end, split down the middle and flattened to form a sheet. Finally, the sheets were carefully packed and transported by cart or boat to the construction site, often many hundreds of miles away.

The glazier would select pieces of glass of the right colour and cut them to shape using a red-hot iron. If the glass was really hard, he would spit on it until it cracked! The edges of the pieces were then nibbled into the exact shape using a tool called a 'grozing iron'. Today, glaziers use modern glasscutters.

After all the pieces had been cut and laid on the drawing, the painting could begin. Medieval glaziers used special brushes made from pig, squirrel or badger bristles, depending on the particular painting effect they wanted to achieve. The paint was made from copper or iron oxide, powdered glass, gum arabic and wine or urine (a young boy's was considered the best!). Sometimes the glaziers would use a wash of paint over an area to create a 3D effect in faces or folds of fabric.

The pieces of glass were then carefully placed over a wood fire inside a kiln, to fix the paint to the glass. The kiln was made out of a tunnel of twigs covered with clay, horse manure and chopped hay.

Glaziers each had their own particular style and way of working. We rarely know their names, but we can often tell which glaziers were responsible for which windows, and the glaziers they were trained or influenced by.

Medieval glaziers used an extremely sharp hand axe to cut the lead calmes to size!

10

Sealing the joins with molten lead solder. Today, we use electric or gas soldering irons. Medieval glaziers heated their tools in a fire to make them hot.

Now the window was ready to be assembled using the lead strips – or 'calmes' – to hold them in place. These were made by laying reeds in a shallow box and pouring molten lead over them. When cool, the lead was cut into thin strips and the reeds removed. Another method was to carve grooves into a long thin bar of lead to create an H-shaped cross-section.

The glass was slotted into the calmes and the joins soldered front and back with molten lead. Sections were held in place on the table with closing nails (or 'clozyngnails' as medieval glaziers called them). Finally, a special cement was rubbed into the lead grooves to make the panels watertight.

Early medieval windows were made in small panels, which were fixed inside an iron framework called an armature. This framework was then attached to a wooden frame in the window opening.

THE STORY OF ENGLISH STAINED GLASS

The story of stained glass in England begins in the Anglo-Saxon period. The oldest stained glass found in this country was discovered at a church in Jarrow near Newcastle, dating back to the 7th to 9th centuries. It would seem that the windows were very small and simply patterned.

Later, the Normans introduced more sophisticated building techniques, which meant they could create significantly larger windows in churches. As a result, stained glass windows became more popular in Europe from the late 11th century onwards.

The earliest windows were relatively simple, often featuring a single character, such as a saint or archbishop, as glaziers began to experiment with this new art form. Another popular early subject was the 'Jesse Tree', a family tree which traced Jesus' ancestors back to Jesse, the father of King David.

As their skills developed, the glaziers began to produce more complicated pictures, with backgrounds, textures and clever use of colours and shapes to tell their stories.

Although windows were becoming larger and larger, the preference for richly coloured glass meant that churches in the 12th and 13th centuries were often quite dark inside. However, the effect of sunlight shining through these beautiful windows must have been awe-inspiring to medieval worshippers. Some people, however, felt that church interiors had become too richly decorated. This led to the development of 'grisaille' in the latter part of the 13th century – an almost clear or very pale green glass.

THE BIBLE IN PICTURES?

It has often been thought that stained glass windows were used to teach ordinary people about the stories in the Bible and the lives of the saints. This was a reasonable idea, as very few people could actually read. Books were expensive, scarce and written in Latin, which only monks and priests could understand.

However, windows didn't necessarily follow a strict order and many parts of a church building were not even accessible to most people. But even if the windows were not used directly as teaching aids, they were constant reminders to people of the key stories and principles of the Christian faith.

ALTERNATC EST VI INVNC SVMI VIT

SCHOL ES

▲ One of Canterbury Cathedral's Miracle Windows: 'Mad' Matilda of Cologne is pictured being beaten and pushed towards the city by two attendants.

During the 14th century, new glass colours were introduced, such as red-brown, leafy green and a soft purple known as 'murrey'. Perhaps the most important development of this century, however, was the discovery of a new technique for staining glass yellow. By painting silver oxide on to the surface of clear glass and then heating it, areas could be coloured from pale yellow to almost orange. This meant that the glazier could paint hair, a halo or a crown directly on to a clear piece of glass, rather than having to cut out lots of separate pieces of glass to achieve the same effect. This saved time and led to more intricate designs.

The Black Death plagues of the mid-14th century affected every area of society and many of the country's finest glass craftsmen died. Those that survived were even more highly valued. Work picked up again as the country recovered and rich people wanted to pay for windows to show their gratitude to God for being spared. Perhaps not surprisingly, the Black Death influenced a lot of the subject matter of windows produced during this period, which often included scenes of death, the consequences of sin and the Last Judgement!

The style of English stained glass windows changed again towards the end of the 15th century, influenced by the popularity of Flemish Renaissance painters from Belgium and Holland. Glaziers made greater use of perspective to give paintings a more realistic look and windows were treated like large canvases rather than individual panels. Elizabethan glaziers used translucent enamel paints, made from ground glass and coloured pigments, which allowed them to paint directly on to glass as if they were painting on to wood or canvas.

The golden age of English stained glass, along with church building in general, came to an abrupt end in the 1530s. When the Pope refused to grant Henry VIII a divorce from his wife, Catherine of Aragon, Henry retaliated by breaking away from the Catholic church and establishing his own 'Church of England'. The King ordered the closing down of all abbeys, monasteries and convents across the country. Many of the finest stained glass windows were destroyed or defaced (often, literally, de-faced!).

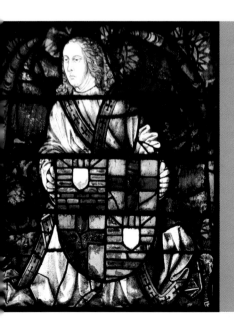

A GIFT IN GLASS

Stained glass windows were expensive and so they were often paid for by rich people in the community. Some wanted their family's coat of arms to be featured in the windows. Many wanted pictures of themselves and their families in the window as a lasting reminder of their generosity.

Apart from reminding the congregation who the rich and powerful in the community were, many donors paid for windows as they believed it would please God, guarantee their place in heaven and encourage future generations to pray for their souls.

This widespread destruction was repeated a century later during the English Civil War.

The Puritans – led by Oliver Cromwell – felt there was too much emphasis on icons and stained glass, and that churches should be as plain and simple as possible. These 'iconoclasts' appointed commissioners who travelled the country, destroying many beautiful stained glass windows. Canterbury escaped relatively lightly, though the Puritan preacher 'Blue Dick' Culmer took great pleasure in smashing the windows with a pike ("...*rattling down proud Becket's glassy bones*", as he called it!).

By the time the monarchy was restored with Charles II, architectural and artistic tastes had moved on. New church designers, such as Sir Christopher Wren, preferred plain glass windows. His masterpiece – St Paul's Cathedral in London, rebuilt after the Great Fire of 1666 – has no stained glass at all.

The fashion for treating glass windows like oil paintings, which began during the Renaissance, continued into the Georgian period. The 19th century saw a growth in religious enthusiasm, increased wealth and a renewed interest in medieval architectural styles. This led, in turn, to a huge increase in demand for 'traditional' stained glass windows. Over 80,000 new windows were made between 1800 and 1900.

In more recent times, glass painters have continued to develop their art. Today, there is often less emphasis on creating actual pictures in stained glass, particularly in modern church buildings. Instead, artists use colour and light to convey meaning, create a mood or to provoke a response – as many forms of modern art attempt to do.

▲ The medieval artist has accurately represented a European, Arab and African in this window... but not the camels!

SIGNS OF THE TIMES

Stained glass windows can tell us a huge amount about daily life in medieval times. Even when illustrating Bible scenes, glaziers painted characters dressed in medieval clothes with fashionable hairstyles of the day. Musical instruments, as well as household items and other everyday objects, would also be easily recognisable to medieval church-goers.

In those days, people enjoyed a strong connection with nature and the land, so windows often featured flowers, plants, trees, crops, birds and animals. Sometimes glaziers had to use their imaginations, as they could not possibly have seen some of the birds and animals they tried to illustrate in the windows. Perhaps that's why some of the more exotic creatures they painted look a little strange. The animals pictured above are supposed to be camels!

A BIT ABOUT BECKET

The murder of Archbishop Thomas Becket in Canterbury Cathedral in 1170 is probably the best known event in the city's history.

In 1154, King Henry II made Thomas his Chancellor – the most powerful official in the kingdom. Thomas certainly had the right skills and experience for the job. He had distinguished himself in battle, was well educated and loved expensive clothes and food.

Henry and Thomas were both strong-willed characters, but they soon became good friends. When Archbishop Theobald died in 1162, King Henry named Thomas as his successor, thinking that it would be a good idea to have *his* man on the inside, so that he could reduce the influence of the church. But Thomas took his new priestly role very seriously and always sided with the church against the king.

Thomas chose to live a simple monastic life, perhaps to make up for all his excesses as Chancellor. He no longer wore lavish clothes and jewellery, but a simple monk's habit over a horse hair shirt, which quickly became infested with lice and fleas. He slept on a cold stone floor and every morning would wash the feet of 13 poor people, feed them and give them money.

King Henry had expected Thomas' full support, but they were always arguing. Things got so bad at one point that the king banished Thomas to France. The final straw came when Thomas excommunicated some of his fellow church leaders for siding with Henry. That meant they could no longer be members of the church, a very serious punishment indeed. When the king heard this, he became extremely angry and four Norman knights – Richard Brito, Hugh de Moreville, Reginald FitzUrse and William de Tracy – pledged to do something about it.

On the evening of 29 December 1170, the four knights confronted Thomas at his house in Palace Street in Canterbury. The frightened monks tried desperately to persuade Thomas to seek sanctuary in the cathedral, but he only did so when he heard Vespers being sung, requiring his attendance. The knights followed Thomas and found him kneeling at the altar and demanded that he pardon the men he had excommunicated. Thomas refused and told the knights that "*for the name of Jesus and the protection of the church, I am ready to embrace death.*"

Seething with anger, the knights struck Thomas three times with their swords. The last blow was so hard that the sword blade snapped in two. One blow sliced off the top of Thomas' head and his blood and brains spilled on to the chapel's stone floor.

Shortly after his violent death, a series of miracles were reported and Thomas was declared a saint by Pope Alexander III three years later. Pilgrims soon began to flock to his shrine in the cathedral. One of them was the king himself, dressed in sackcloth and walking barefoot, repenting for the terrible deed he had caused to happen.

▶ This famous window shows St Thomas. It may look like a medieval window, but it was made in the 20th century!

16

CANTERBURY CATHEDRAL'S STAINED GLASS

Canterbury Cathedral has one of the finest collections of stained glass in the country... largely due to the brutal murder of its archbishop and a few stray sparks!

After Thomas Becket's murder in the cathedral in 1170 and subsequent reports of miraculous healings in his name, his shrine became one of the most important places of pilgrimage outside of the Holy Land.

But disaster struck in 1174, when one of the houses near the cathedral gate caught fire.

"On the fifth of September, in the year of grace 1174, about 9 o'clock, the wind blowing from the south with a fury almost beyond conception, a fire broke out... Thus the house of God, hitherto a paradise of pleasure, then lay contemptible in the ashes of the fire... The grief of the sons of the Church was so great that they howled rather than sang Matins and Vespers..."

▲ An eyewitness account by Brother Gervase, a monk at Canterbury

Although it was quickly brought under control, sparks were carried up on to the wooden roof of the cathedral and the whole of Archbishop Anselm's recently completed choir building was destroyed.

Thanks to its highly profitable pilgrim trade, the cathedral's monks could afford to rebuild the eastern end of the church and fill it with the very best stained glass. They appointed the famous French architect William of Sens to supervise the rebuilding of the new choir. William was eager to use the new Gothic style of architecture that was becoming popular in Europe. With pillars, vaulting and flying buttresses bearing the weight of the roof, more of the wall space could be taken up by windows.

▲ Jonah is thrown overboard and is swallowed by a whale in this panel from one of the Bible Windows.

Unfortunately, William would never see his masterpiece completed. He fell off the scaffolding during the building's construction and was taken back to France, where he died. His work was finished by William the Englishman.

Medieval windows always followed similar patterns. The same themes were used in cathedrals throughout Europe, but interpreted slightly differently by each glazier. Stained glass was expensive and little went to waste – small pieces of glass left over after the main pictures had been made were saved and used in borders and backgrounds of other windows.

Canterbury Cathedral's stained glass windows can be divided into six main groups:

1 **Saints Windows**: each of the altars dedicated to saints had its own window. Only St Martin's, in the north east transept, remains. There are also two sets of windows dedicated to former archbishops who were created saints: St Dunstan and St Alphege, each of whom had a shrine beside the high altar. They are located in the north choir aisle.

2 **Genealogy Windows**: 86 seated figures from Adam to Christ, half of which are still in the cathedral. There is also a Jesse Tree window, which illustrates this in a different way, but only two of the original panels now remain.

3 **Bible Windows**: illustrating stories from the Old and New Testaments. Three windows remain out of the original 12 – in the north choir aisle and Corona Chapel.

4 **Miracle Windows**: one of Canterbury's most important set of windows, illustrating the miracles attributed to St Thomas Becket. They are located in the Trinity Chapel.

5 **Royal Windows**: the main focus of the west window was originally the English kings, though only eight survive today. The Royal Window in the north-west transept shows the kneeling figures of King Edward IV and his queen, Elizabeth Woodville, together with their surviving children. Alongside is a memorial to King George VI and a commemoration of the coronation of Queen Elizabeth II.

6 **Modern Windows**: Canterbury Cathedral has a number of 20th century stained glass windows. They include stunning creations by three important stained glass artists, Christopher Whall, Ervin Bossanyi and Harry Stammers.

FINDING YOUR WAY AROUND

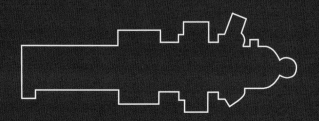

The small maps on the following pages will help you locate the windows in the cathedral. You may also find the plan of the cathedral and its windows in the inside back cover useful as you wander round.

SAINTS WINDOWS

In the small triforium windows above the choir aisles, the monks were reminded of the lives of two former archbishops, St Dunstan and St Alphege, to whom altars in the presbytery were dedicated.

ST DUNSTAN

The windows show two scenes from St Dunstan's colourful life. The first illustrates an event which took place in his early days in Glastonbury, when he was prevented from entering the church to pray by a demon. He climbed up on to the roof, and was carried down to the altar by an angel!

The second window shows St Dunstan at the Conference of Calne. The meeting took place in an upstairs room and, as his opponents criticised the archbishop, part of the floor gave way and they crashed to the floor below. Miraculously, St Dunstan and his companions were unharmed!

▼ Detail from window showing a demon and St Dunstan being rescued by an angel.

ST ALPHEGE

In 1011, the vikings landed at Sandwich and laid siege to Canterbury, demanding the cathedral's treasures. The citizens defended the walled city for nearly three weeks before the vikings finally broke in and set fire to the cathedral and most of the houses. Many people were killed and Archbishop Alphege and other church leaders were taken hostage.

St Alphege pleaded with the citizens of Canterbury not to pay any ransom for him and, seven months later, he was killed at a drunken feast in London. He was named a saint for this brave and selfless act, becoming the cathedral's first Christian martyr.

▲ The siege of Canterbury by the vikings.

▼ St Alphege is killed with an axe. Some historians believe he died after being pelted with oxbones.

21

GENEALOGY WINDOWS

In the medieval period, Canterbury Cathedral was a monastic community and a local church. The content of its windows, and their location in the building, reflect this.

Only the monks had access to the choir, where they conducted their eight daily services of sung psalms and prayers. Here the monks could look up at the choir clerestory windows and contemplate Jesus' ancestors.

This series of paired figures began on the north side with God the Creator and Adam and finished on the south side with the Virgin Mary and Jesus himself. All except Adam are seated. The figures are the work of more than one glazier and probably took around 20 years to complete.

Only around half of the original 86 figures have survived. Some of these are still located in the clerestory; others were moved to fill gaps in the great west window and in windows in the south west transept.

The line of clerestory windows are separated by two huge circular 'oculus' windows, each around 4.5m in diameter and located opposite each other in the north east and south east transepts. They are designed to illustrate the Old and New Testament law.

▲ According to the Bible, Methuselah was the oldest person ever to live. He was the grandfather of Noah, and died at the age of 969!

◄ This picture of Adam digging in the Garden of Eden is the oldest of the Genealogy Windows and the only one showing a figure standing up. It is located in the West Window.

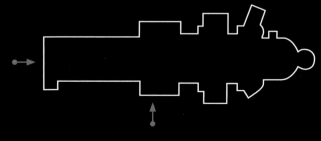

THE JESSE TREE WINDOW

The Jesse Tree was another popular medieval design for illustrating Jesus' ancestors. Sadly, only two panels survived destruction by the Puritans. They are installed in the window on the far left of the Corona Chapel, which was built to house a saintly relic – the crown (or corona) of St Thomas Becket's head, which had been cut off by his murderers.

The lower panel shows King Josiah. Above, seated and crowned, is the Virgin Mary.

BIBLE WINDOWS

There were originally 12 round-headed Bible Windows, located in the choir aisles and the two eastern transepts. Only a small number of panels from this part of the cathedral now remain.

Each window contains panels arranged in groups of three: one New Testament scene in the middle and two Old Testament ones either side, echoing its theme(s). They are known as 'typological' windows.

The series began at the west end of the north choir aisle with the angel's visit to the Virgin Mary (the annunciation) and Jesus' birth and ended at the west end of the south choir aisle with Jesus' resurrection.

The Bible windows were made at the end of the 12th century, when the choir was being rebuilt following the 1174 fire. Many of the windows were later destroyed by the Puritans in the 1640s. What was left of the panels was gathered together to create these three windows, which continue into the Corona Chapel at the far eastern end of the cathedral.

Bible Window 1 originally contained scenes from Jesus' childhood running down the middle. Window 2 contained scenes of Jesus

in the temple, his baptism and his three temptations in the wilderness.

The Redemption Window in the centre of the Corona Chapel is also part of the Bible Window series. The theme of this window is Jesus' death and resurrection.

The next few pages contain some sample scenes from the three Bible Windows. You can download a complete list from our website: **www.paintingsinlight.co.uk**.

▼ The parable of the sower: the seed falls on stony ground and is eaten by birds.

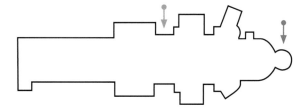

◄ The Jesse Tree window is located in the Corona Chapel.

Window 1, Row 3: theme: giving of gifts (*left to right*)

THE QUEEN OF SHEBA PRESENTS GIFTS TO KING SOLOMON
(2 Chronicles 9:1)

King Solomon, left, is seated on his throne greeting the Queen of Sheba. Two attendants on camels bring gifts to Solomon and the (green!) camel's head behind them suggests there are more to come.

THE NATIVITY (Matthew 2:1–11)

The three wise men and the shepherds present their gifts at the stable. The wise men, on the left, offer their gifts to the baby Jesus, who raises his hand as a sign of blessing. Above them is the star that has also brought the shepherds. They are barefoot and carry staves.

This is probably the earliest recorded nativity

scene showing wise men and shepherds worshipping the baby Jesus. However, in the Bible, they are two separate events, many months apart!

JOSEPH'S BROTHERS COME TO EGYPT TO BUY CORN
(Genesis 43:15)

Joseph sits on his throne with his brothers on one side and the Egyptians on the other holding bowls of coins brought by Joseph's family to pay for food.

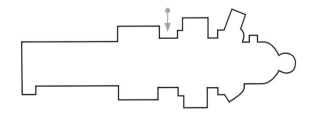

HIDDEN MEANINGS

Like all typological windows, this series of panels illustrates a New Testament story – in this case, the nativity – and pairs it with stories from the Old Testament that mirror or point to that event. But the pictures contain deeper theological and moral meanings too.

King Solomon, Jesus and Joseph are all sitting on thrones with footstalls, indicating their authority. The Queen of Sheba recognises Solomon's authority by bringing him gifts. Similarly, the wise men recognise Jesus as Saviour and offer him gifts, while the curious shepherds look on. Joseph's status is recognised by the Egyptians, but not by his own family, the Israelites, who sold him into slavery. The hidden meaning here is Jesus' acceptance by the Gentiles but rejection by the Jews, a common theme which runs through many of the scenes in this Bible Window.

Window 2, Row 2: theme: the number six

THE WEDDING AT CANA
(John 2:1–10)

This panel celebrates Jesus' first recorded miracle, when he turned water into wine at a wedding in Cana. Jesus is seated at the right end of the table with Mary his mother and a disciple (wearing halos!). At the other end sits the governor of the feast. Between them are the bride and groom. In the foreground are six water pots. A servant is carrying a bowl of wine from these to the table, while another servant refills them with water. Water transformed into wine was a symbol of how belief in Jesus would change sinners' lives. Can you count how many times the theme of 'six' appears in this row?

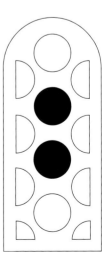

Window 2, Row 3: theme: redemption

THE MIRACULOUS CATCH OF FISH
(Luke 5:4–9)

Jesus sits in the boat on the left with his disciples Simon and Andrew. In the other boat are James and John. Between them is a net full of fish after Jesus has told his disciples where to find them. After this miracle Jesus gave Simon the name Peter, which means 'rock' in Greek (we'd probably call him Rocky!). This panel was originally paired with pictures of Peter converting the Gentiles and Peter preaching to the Jews, with the theme of redemption.

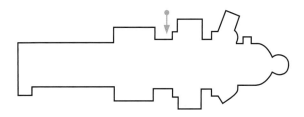

Redemption Window, Row 3: theme: resurrection (*left to right*)

NOAH IN THE ARK (Genesis 8:6–11)
After 40 days in the ark, Noah releases a dove to see if there is any dry land. The dove returns with an olive leaf.

THE RESURRECTION
(Matthew 28:1–10; Mark 16:1–18;
John 20:1–31)

Jesus emerges triumphant from the tomb, with an angel standing either side.

MICHAL AND DAVID
(1 Samuel 19:8–18)
David's wife Michal lowers him out of a window to help him escape from Saul, who wants to kill him.

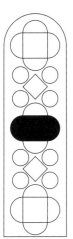

The Redemption Window illustrates the five stages in Jesus' Passion: crucifixion, entombment, resurrection, ascension and reigning in glory, paired with Old Testament stories with similar themes.

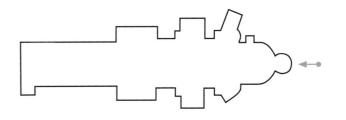

The town of Sodom is burned to the ground because of its sin, while Lot's family is led to safety by two angels. Disobeying God's instructions, Lot's wife looks back and is turned into a pillar of salt.

MIRACLE WINDOWS

Probably the most amazing of all Canterbury Cathedral's windows are those that the pilgrims first encountered as they entered the Trinity Chapel to visit St Thomas' shrine. Here the pilgrims were clearly reminded why they had travelled all this way – because praying to God through St Thomas brought about miracles!

In medieval times, people believed much more in miracles than they do today and would ask their favourite saints to support them when praying to God for help or healing.

These Miracle Windows, located in at the eastern end of the cathedral, tell the stories of people from all walks of life – from a peasant boy to a king. All have been helped in some way by praying to St Thomas.

The stories told in the Miracle Windows are based on reports written by two Canterbury monks, Benedict and William, in the three years following St Thomas' murder.

All the windows have Latin inscriptions, which the vast majority of people would not have been able to read. It is likely that monk guides explained the pictures to the visiting pilgrims, just as cathedral guides do for visitors today.

Only seven out of the original 12 windows remain. King Henry VIII put an end to the 'cult of St Thomas', as he called it, and made sure the saint's image was obliterated when he destroyed his beautiful shrine.

The stories these windows tell, and the pictures they contain, give us a fascinating insight into medieval life. The conditions shown include leprosy, plague, typhoid, madness, toothache, swollen feet, epilepsy, blindness and lameness. We also see some of the treatments given, and the rough justice system of the day!

You can read a few of these miraculous stories on the following pages. A complete list can be downloaded from our website at: **www.paintingsinlight.co.uk**.

▾ William of Kellett is at work when his axe slips, badly injuring his leg. Can you see the pool of blood at his feet and the faces of his horrified friends?

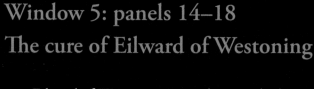

Window 5: panels 14–18
The cure of Eilward of Westoning

Eilward of Westoning is owed money by his neighbour, Fulk. When Fulk doesn't pay up, Eilward takes a pair of gloves and a sharpening stone from him (14).

Eilward is brought before the magistrate and found guilty of theft. He is pinned to the ground by a plank while his accusers gouge out his eyes and castrate him (15).

While lying in bed recovering from his ordeal, St Thomas appears and touches Eilward's forehead and eye sockets with his staff. Eilward's eyes regrow (17)!

He shows his healed eyes to other pilgrims, who give him coins. Eilward donates the money to a crippled beggar (16). Finally, we see him giving thanks at St Thomas' tomb (18).

17

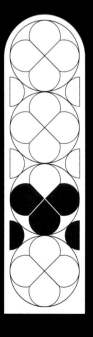

H PVNTV ECTAS VNTLVMI H.MEM RRARESECTA

NST ATRIDM VASINIS RA

AS ATHARR ANTIPOPVLVS
MA GNAL IASANCTI

Window 6: panels 13–15
The drowning of Robert (Bobby) of Rochester

Robert of Rochester, known to his friends as Bobby, is a disobedient and naughty boy of eight. He goes to play down by the River Medway and he and his friends throw stones at some frogs. Tragically, Bobby falls into the river and drowns (13). His young companions run to tell Bobby's parents (14). A man with a long pole drags the boy's lifeless body out of the river and his mother opens her arms to receive it (15). Bobby is hung upside down and rolled in a tub, but can't be revived.

His mother measures him and offers to St Thomas an equal length of silver wire if he recovers. He does!

MIE ... A R EVE ISL... DEFVNCTVM/ZENTSPISCANTVIINRIREPENTES

15

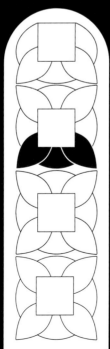

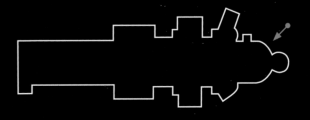

PROFERT GHI F BR SIOTTVMC VNPHHTEK NOS

GHVIVS H CCEDIT VO A MVNDVM R
ECOBEU NAR

VIN DIC TEM O LES DOM VS E G VA 7 MOR TV A PRO

MVRIL IS FVNV SRELIQVIS VAFI SGRI MINATVR

PERG V LITVR PVE RZ M ODIT VR PLANCTV SGEM

Window 6: panels 25–33
Plague in the house of Sir Jordan Fitz-Eisulf

Sir Jordan Fitz-Eisulf was a knight. His story begins with the funeral of the family's nurse, who has died from the plague. When it looks like his younger son is about to die too, Sir Jordan manages to revive him with holy water brought by pilgrims from St Thomas' tomb. He vows to make a thank offering, but fails to do so, even when reminded of his debt by a blind and lame beggar, who saw St Thomas in a vision. His elder son is then struck down with the plague and dies.

Sir Jordan and his family finally go on a pilgrimage to Canterbury, where they pile gold and silver at the saint's tomb to pay their debt.

Can you work out the correct order of the panels?

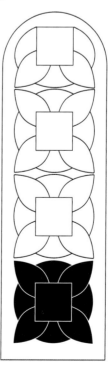

39

Window 12: panels 1–6
Baby Geoffrey of Winchester

Poor little baby Geoffrey of Winchester!
First we see him dying of fever in his
cradle while his mother and grandmother
look anxiously on. Then St Thomas
appears with a book under his arm and
a hand raised in blessing. The baby
gets better and his family make a thank
offering at St Thomas' tomb.

But tragedy strikes poor Geoffrey and
his family again – a wall crashes down
on to his cradle (3)! His mother and
grandmother pray to the saint, while
Geoffrey's distraught father sits head in
hands amongst the rubble.

His mother faints and a servant tries to
revive her with water. Another servant
starts to carefully dig out the rubble with
a pickaxe (6). Miraculously, baby Geoffrey
is found smiling and unharmed (5)!

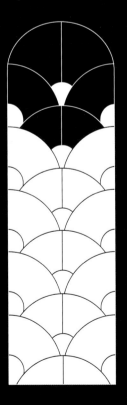

LD RAZ&. PRIVSLVN ESED VARFRI

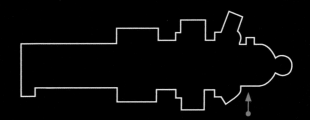

ROYAL WINDOWS

The cathedral's original nave and transepts, which had survived the fire of 1174, were rebuilt in the late 14th century. The king, Richard II, helped pay for the work, as did a number of other wealthy people. Only two windows remain from this set – the west window and the north-west transept window – and both have royal themes.

The west window stands above the main entrance to the nave, though you are more likely to enter the cathedral today by the south-west door. At the very top are the coats of arms of Richard II and his two wives. Below are images of apostles and prophets.

Originally this window featured the early English kings, including Canute, Edward the Confessor and William the Conqueror. Only eight remain today. The gaps have been filled with some of Jesus' ancestors from the genealogical windows designed for the choir clerestory.

The second of the Royal-themed windows is in the north-west transept. This dates from the late 15th century and shows the kneeling figures of King Edward IV and his queen, Elizabeth Woodville, together with their two sons and five daughters. The two princes – Edward V and Richard, Duke of

York – were imprisoned in the Tower of London after their father's death and became known as the 'Princes in the Tower'. They died in mysterious circumstances soon after. Many believe they were murdered by their uncle Richard, Duke of Gloucester. He was next in line to the throne after them, and became King Richard III. In 2013, his long lost remains were found under a car park in Leicester!

Edward's eldest daughter Elizabeth, also shown in the window, later became Queen of England, as the wife of King Henry VII, Richard's successor.

This window overlooks the spot where St Thomas Becket was murdered. It used to feature scenes of Jesus' crucifixion and the Virgin Mary, as well as a life-size figure of the saint himself, before it was largely destroyed by the Puritans in 1643.

Alongside is a more modern Royal window – a memorial to King George VI and a commemoration of the coronation of Queen Elizabeth II. It features members of the current Royal family, as well as state and church officials who attended the coronation (pictured overleaf).

▸ Edward IV was king of England twice, winning the 'Wars of the Roses' against the Lancastrians to establish the House of York on the English throne.

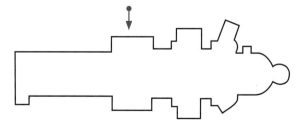

◂ The three younger daughters of Edward IV: Anne, Catherine and Bridget.

'MODERN' WINDOWS

Canterbury Cathedral is famous for its medieval stained glass windows, but it also has a number of important modern ones too. They include windows designed by the 20th century stained glass artists, Christopher Whall, Ervin Bossanyi and Harry Stammers.

Sadly, a number of the cathedral's windows were destroyed during World War II, including two windows made by Christopher Whall, a member of the so-called 'Arts and Crafts' movement. This movement was started by William Morris in the late 19th century to promote traditional craftsmanship using simple shapes, often decorated with medieval, romantic or folk designs.

Fortunately, another of Christopher's beautiful windows survives in the south-west transept. It features scenes of the nativity, Jesus' agony in the garden of Gethsemane and his resurrection. Whall used a newly developed glass known as 'Early English Slab', which is thicker and more uneven than medieval glass.

But it is in the south-east transept that you will find the cathedral's most surprising modern windows: four pictures by Hungarian artist Ervin Bossanyi, based on the themes of salvation and peace.

◀ Queen Elizabeth II at her coronation, with Prince Philip, Prince Charles and Princess Anne.

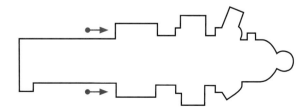

▶ Uriel, the bringer of light: a detail from Christopher Whall's window in the south-west transept.

▶ Ervin Bossanyi's
colourful window
based on the
theme of peace.

Ervin came to England in the 1930s to escape Nazi persecution in his own country. Although his figures appear almost cartoon-like, look closely at them and you will see how sophisticated and beautifully made they are.

In St Anselm's Chapel is a vividly coloured window by another well known 20th century glass painter, Harry Stammers. In addition to St Anselm, the window features Archbishop Lanfranc, his doctor Baldwin, King William Rufus and King Henry I.

In the cloisters, you will find a window featuring Pope Gregory, who sent Augustine on a mission to Canterbury in 597 to restore Christianity to pagan Britain. He is pictured with the first four Archbishops of Canterbury.

A window in the west walk features the musicians Henry Purcell, John Marbeke and Thomas Tallis alongside Archbishop Stephen Langton. The window alongside was installed in memory of Dean Richard Lawrie Sheppard and features the adoration of the shepherds, St Francis, St Martin... and a pious pelican! One of the shepherds is Dean Sheppard himself... a joke on his name!

The Chapter House has two large windows. The 1896 east window shows English monarchs and archbishops of Canterbury, from Queen Bertha and St Augustine in the sixth century to Queen Victoria and Archbishop Benson in the 19th century.

▸ St Anselm is the centrepiece of Harry Stammers' vividly coloured window.

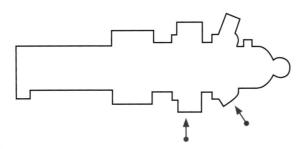

47

RESTORATION -
A FAMILY BUSINESS

The story of stained glass restoration at Canterbury Cathedral goes back to 1819, when architect George Austin was appointed Surveyor to the Fabric. His family would look after the cathedral's stained glass for the next 133 years.

George Austin handed on the work to his son George Junior in 1848, before the business passed to his nephew Samuel Caldwell in 1862, and then to his son, Samuel Junior, in 1906. Samuel Junior (*pictured above*) eventually retired in 1952, aged 93!

George Austin Senior developed a keen interest in the cathedral's stained glass windows and became an expert painter,

despite having no previous experience. He replaced pieces of worn or broken glass with new pieces that he painted himself, matching as carefully as possible the style of the original. George would use medieval glass pieces from other windows to make his repairs and developed techniques to make new glass look much older.

His son, George Austin Junior, took a different approach. He saw the importance of preserving the original glass as much as possible. His biggest challenge was the lack of suitable replacement glass to match with the original. Sometimes he would replace whole panels with new glass if it was difficult to achieve a close enough match. He rarely threw away pieces of old glass, however small, in case they might be useful in future restoration projects. Enough of George Austin Junior's work still survives today for us to appreciate his craftsmanship and his thoughtful approach to ancient glass.

Later in the 19th century, people's attitude towards medieval glass started to change. They began to appreciate imperfections in the glass and signs of age. Samuel Caldwell Senior was strongly influenced by this and began to sort and store pieces of medieval glass by colour. He invented new methods for cleaning and repainting the pieces so that they could be reused.

His son, Samuel Caldwell Junior, took great pride in producing almost perfect forgeries of medieval glass, recreating lost scenes with his own designs and even painting on artificial corrosion to make the glass look more authentic. Most people find it hard to tell the difference between the original medieval designs and those Samuel Caldwell Junior produced many hundreds of years later!

When Samuel Caldwell Junior retired, his workshop was taken over by George Easton, his assistant for many years. He continued the traditions established by the Austin/Caldwell family.

In 1973, a new conservation studio was established at Canterbury Cathedral, with a very different approach to conservation and restoration.

▶ A glazier carefully reconstructs one of the Bible windows in the cathedral's stained glass studio in the 1950s. The restored top panel is to his left.

ELEGERVNT · STEPHANVM · VIRVM · PLENVM · FIDE

▸ Workmen remove the panels
from the South Oculus
window for conservation.

CONSERVATION –
A NEW APPROACH

The damaging effects of wind, rain, condensation, frost, heat and pollution will eventually destroy stained glass windows. Today's stained glass conservation team concentrates on preserving the original medieval glass and protecting it from these harmful elements.

Panels are carefully removed from the window frame then photographed to record their condition before conservation. A rubbing is taken of the leaded lines to create a full-size copy of the panel. A conservator then marks this up with the condition of each piece of glass and prepares a report with their recommendations for conserving the panel.

Next, the panel is carefully cleaned using a damp cotton bud and a tiny sable brush, with the aid of a microscope if necessary. Harder bits are removed with a scalpel. It's a very delicate and time-consuming process. Once the panel has been cleaned, the repair work can begin.

Loose paint is repaired using microscopic dots of a special glue. Glass is never repainted now, as it would destroy its historical value. Sometimes missing letters of inscriptions are restored by painting them on to a thin piece of clear glass and attaching this to the back of the original, so that the words can be read.

The lead calmes are rarely replaced these days, unless they are so fragile that they make the panel unstable. All the glass at Canterbury has been re-leaded at least once over the past 200 years, so none of the original medieval lead remains.

Once the repairs have been carried out, the panels are photographed again and a final report is produced.

To protect the window from further environmental damage, a simplified duplicate is created using clear glass. This is installed in place of the original window, which is reinstalled a few centimetres in front. The air gap between the two prevents condensation from forming on the medieval glass.

The original window is now protected from the harmful effects of the weather and pollutants and can continue to be enjoyed by future generations for many more years.

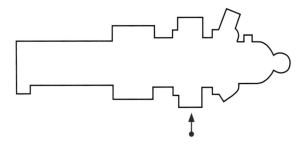

▲ Left: a medieval panel after 800 years of ageing.
Right: how it would have looked when first installed.

①

②

③

CONSERVATION IN ACTION

1 Removing the stained glass panel from its frame.
2 Photographing a panel before conservation.
3 Making a rubbing to create a full-sized copy of the leading.
4 Preparing a condition report.
5 Cleaning the panel.
6 Sealing the cracked pieces of glass with glue.
7 Creating the leading for the protective clear panel.
8 Installing the protective clear panel in the window frame.
9 Installing the repaired panel and metal supporting frame.

⑥

⑧

⑨

ACKNOWLEDGEMENTS

I'm eternally grateful to Léonie Seliger at Canterbury Cathedral's stained glass conservation studio for her assistance in supplying photographs and checking the text, as well as her patience and willingness in helping a novice understand the intricacies and beauty of medieval stained glass.

I would like to thank Professor Bob Newport at the University of Kent for his input on the chapter on glass, and for his enthusiasm for the subject that triggered mine, and Fiona Gifford, for her proof-reading and insightful comments. I would also like to thank Andrew Edwards, Chief Executive of the Canterbury Cathedral Trust, for allowing me to embark on this adventure by securing funding, and to the sponsors – the Dr Mortimer and Theresa Sackler Foundation and the World Monuments Fund – without whose generous contribution this book would not have been published.

Finally, a big thank you to all the authors who have been equally inspired to tell the story of Canterbury Cathedral's amazing stained glass and whose works provided me with invaluable source material. Their respective titles are listed in the bibliography on the right. Do read them if you want to find out more!

PHOTO CREDITS

I have done my best to trace all the respective copyright holders of the illustrations and photographs used in this book and apologise for any errors or omissions. I would be happy to correct these on the next reprint. Thank you to the copyright holders below who have kindly allowed me to use their images:

Dean and Chapter of Canterbury Cathedral: front cover and pages 3, 8, 9, 10, 11, 12, 13, 14, 15, 20, 21, 22, 23, 24, 25, 30, 31, 32, 33, 34, 35, 36, 37, 38, 39, 40, 41, 42, 43, 44, 48, 49, 50, 51, 52, 53, inside back cover (plan) and back cover.

Sonia Halliday or Sonia Halliday and Laura Lushingham: pages 18, 28, 29, 56 and 57.

Shutterstock Inc: pages 4, 5, 6 and 7.

Ingram Image Ltd: page 18 top, flap (stonework) and inside back cover (compass).

Martyn Barr: pages 17 and 47.

Angelo Hornak: page 46.

Roger Hutchins (c) Dorling Kindersley: inside front cover.

BIBLIOGRAPHY

English Stained Glass by Painton Cowen. Published by Thames & Hudson Limited, 2008. ISBN: 978 0 500 23846 2.

Glass: A Short History by David Whitehouse. Published by The British Museum Press, 2012. ISBN 978 0 7141 5086 4.

The History of Glass by Dan Klein and Ward Lloyd. Published by under the Black Cat imprint by MacDonald & Co (Publishers) Ltd, 1992. ISBN 978 0 7481 0246 4.

The Medieval Windows of Canterbury Cathedral by Sue Earlam. Published by the Dean and Chapter, Canterbury Cathedral, 1995.

The Miracle Windows by Jane Stenson. Published by the Dean and Chapter, Canterbury Cathedral, 1987.

Stained Glass by Roger Rosewell. Published by Shire Publications Ltd, 2012. ISBN 978 0 74781 147 3.

Stained Glass in Canterbury Cathedral by Sarah Brown. Published by Cathedral Gifts Ltd, 1995. ISBN 978 0 90621131 1.

Stained Glass of Canterbury Cathedral by Paul M.A. Michael. Published by Scala, 2004. ISBN 9781857593655.